The Campfire Leader

Igniting Trust, Influence, and Leadership That Lasts

By Rob Jackson

Dedication

I want to dedicate this book to my family and friends who encouraged me to write this follow-up. Their support enabled me to continue sharing the Campfire Leadership Philosophy and allows me to live out my mantra to "Change the world and not just play the game." Their backing has made me more confident and achieve things that I never imagined were possible.

Foreword

"I have known Rob Jackson for over 17 years and found his leadership advice most valuable. Rob worked in the corporate world for many years and turned his expertise into workshops that help individuals and groups. He shares leadership and professional development principles with individuals from various socioeconomic backgrounds. Over the years, his insight has proven successful in my career, among colleagues, and onboard Team members.

I have recommended Rob to many colleagues and business professionals. *The Campfire Leader* is an excellent resource for continued learning and development."

- Cruise ship Captain Johannes Tysse

Before You Start Reading

This isn't just a book about leadership.

It's about trust.
It's about influence.

It's about becoming the kind of leader people *choose* to follow—even when they don't have to.

Whether you're here out of curiosity, growth, burnout, or ambition, you're holding more than chapters. You're holding a compass.

The stories, tools, and insights inside are meant to meet you where you are—and help you become who you're meant to be. Take your time. Mark the margins. Share the moments that hit home. This is your fire to tend.

If the message resonates at any point, or you'd like to explore it further—whether through coaching, workshops, or a conversation—I'd love to connect.

Visit **magnovo.com** or **campfireleadership.com**

 Or, email me personally at **rob.jackson@magnovo.com**

Now, let's light the first spark.

Table of Contents

Chapter 1 – The Warmth of the Campfire

Campfire Leadership Glossary of Terms

Before we dive into the warmth of the campfire, it's important to establish a shared language.
This glossary will help you navigate the terms used throughout the Campfire Leadership philosophy, so you can better understand yourself and those you lead.

Campfire Leader
A well-balanced leader who adapts across all four DISC-based leadership styles. They inspire, connect, and empower—like a fire that invites people in without burning them out.

Torch Leader
A calm, dependable leader who provides quiet strength. Torch Leaders are the emotional anchors of a team, leading through loyalty, patience, and consistency.

Spotlight Leader
Bold, decisive, and action-oriented. Spotlight Leaders thrive in high-stakes environments and push teams toward results—but need to strike a balance between intensity and empathy.

Disco Light Leader
Energetic, enthusiastic, and people-driven. These leaders inspire and motivate through charisma, but must be mindful of overcommitting or avoiding difficult conversations.

Lighthouse Leader
Strategic, thoughtful, and precise. Lighthouse Leaders guide others through data, planning, and systems. They shine brightly in chaos but can become rigid under stress.

Spark
A moment of inspiration or clarity that ignites new energy, ideas, or direction.

Fuel
The people, values, and principles that keep your leadership energy going.

Oxygen
Space for creativity, reflection, and breathing room.

The Fire
The culture, trust, and shared mission you create as a leader.

Burnout
When the fire consumes rather than sustains. A signal that your resources are depleted.

Campfire Conversations
Intentional discussions designed to build trust, spark growth, or deepen team dynamics.

Flame Tending
The act of checking in, adjusting your approach, and taking care of your team.

Leadership Compass
Your internal guide—your core values, style tendencies, and long-term vision.

About the Workbook & Journal

Located at the back of this book, the *Campfire Leadership Workbook & Journal* is your hands-on companion to bring these ideas to life.

Inside, you'll find a leadership style quiz, guided journaling prompts, weekly reflection spaces, a 6-month leadership challenge series, and practical tools to track your progress and monitor your mental well-being.

Whether used privately or in team discussions, this workbook will help you develop your leadership presence and live out the Campfire Philosophy.

Welcome to the Fire

There's something inherently comforting about a campfire. It draws people in with its warmth, its glow, its ability to make a stranger feel like part of a circle. It's the place where stories are told, songs are sung, and wisdom is passed down. Campfires don't command attention—they invite it. And just like the campfire, the best leaders are those who radiate light without demanding the spotlight.

The Campfire Leadership Philosophy was born from this idea: that leadership isn't a title or a throne to sit on, it's a fire to tend. It's not about control, it's about connection. A great leader understands when to shine, when to reflect, when to illuminate a path, and when to be still and let others shine.

The Campfire Leader doesn't burn people with power. They warm people with presence.

Imagine four different kinds of leaders, each with their own strengths and quirks.

- The **Torch Leader** lights the way. They are steady, dependable, and the picture of consistency. People feel safe walking beside them.
- The **Disco Ball Leader** spins excitement and energy. They inspire, uplift, and bring charisma to every situation.
- The **Spotlight Leader** commands attention. They're direct, decisive, and driven by results. They know where to go and make sure everyone else knows, too.
- The **Lighthouse Leader** offers guidance from a distance. They are wise, strategic, and always watching from the shore.

A Campfire Leader, though, doesn't choose just one of these traits—they balance all four.

They know when to switch gears, when to take the lead, when to step back, and when to let someone else take over control.

The Day I Learned This Lesson

Let me tell you a story.

I began my leadership career in my early 20's as the mailroom supervisor of a credit card processing company in Salinas, California.

I thought leadership meant having all the answers. I wore my "boss" title like a badge and gave orders with pride. But something didn't feel right. People did what I asked, sure, but they didn't seem inspired. They weren't growing. They weren't contributing ideas. They weren't lighting up.

One day, a younger team member named Jenna came to me with a suggestion. I nodded, dismissed it quickly, and moved on. She nodded back, but her spark dimmed. A week later, she quit.

That moment still haunts me to this day.

At the time, I did not comprehend it; however, I later realized that I wasn't tending the fire. I was trying to hold a torch, but it was blinding people. I had ignored the warmth that authentic leadership brings. I had mistaken being "in charge" for being impactful. Jenna taught me that people don't follow titles. They follow trust, warmth, and authenticity.

That negative experience sparked my desire to become a better listener and leader, and it set me on the path to becoming a Campfire Leader.

The Philosophy in Practice

Campfire Leadership isn't a theory—it's a way of being.

When you're in a room, do people tend to relax or become tense? Do they speak more or less? Do they lean in or check out? Your presence as a leader should invite others to be themselves. It should be safe, steady, and just challenging enough to spark growth.

Every great campfire requires three things:

- **Fuel** – The people, their passions, their personalities.
- **Oxygen** – The space to breathe, think, create, and speak.
- **Spark** – The leader who lights it all up with vision and clarity.

The Campfire Leader doesn't take credit for the fire; they tend to it, protect it, and keep it going.

Why This Book Exists

This book is for those who:

- Are tired of outdated leadership models.
- They want to connect more than they command.
- Believe that warmth and wisdom can coexist with results and responsibility.

We'll explore each leadership style in the coming chapters—Torch, Disco Light, Spotlight, and Lighthouse—and then learn how to integrate them into your Campfire Leadership Style.

You don't have to be the loudest voice in the room. You don't have to be the smartest. You just have to be the leader who builds a fire worth gathering around.

So, pull up a seat.
Grab a log.
And let's build something unforgettable.

Chapter 2 – The Torch Leader: Steady in the Storm

"Success is the sum of small efforts, repeated day in and day out."
—Robert Collier

If there were ever a symbol of dependable leadership, it's the torch. It doesn't flicker wildly or blind with brightness. It burns consistently, steadily, and reliably.

The **Torch Leader** is the one that others follow into the unknown. They aren't flashy. They don't seek applause. But when things go sideways, plans fall apart, or emotions run high, everyone turns to the Torch. Why? Because they're a calming force. They don't overreact; they respond.

Who Is the Torch Leader?

In the DISC personality framework, this is your **Steady (S)** leader. Torch Leaders are:

- Calm under pressure
- Loyal and dependable
- Great listeners
- Team-oriented
- Patient and supportive

They provide reliable support that others can depend on. They are often the glue holding the team together, especially when chaos threatens to pull it apart.

But Torch Leaders don't get enough credit. Because they're not loud or dominant, they can be overlooked. Their leadership doesn't come with a megaphone—it comes with a steady hand and quiet confidence.

Strengths of a Torch Leader

1. **Loyal** – They stick by their people and causes.
2. **Supportive** – They lift others without needing to be seen.
3. **Consistent** – You always know what to expect.
4. **Patient** – They allow others the time to grow and learn.
5. **Calm** – Even in crisis, they breathe slowly and think clearly.
6. **Collaborative** – They prioritize teamwork over ego.
7. **Empathetic** – They care deeply about the people they lead.
8. **Balanced** – They don't overpromise or underdeliver.
9. **Reliable** – You can always count on them.
10. **Protective** – They watch out for the team's well-being.
11. **Encouraging** – They motivate without pressure.
12. **Grounded** – They don't get swept up in drama.
13. **Loyal to Values** – They stay true to what matters.
14. **Servant-hearted** – They lead by serving.
15. **Thoughtful** – They pause and consider before they act.

Opportunities for a Torch Leader

1. **Conflict-avoidant** – They may hesitate to address tension.
2. **Too passive** – They can be overshadowed by louder voices.
3. **Resistant to change** – They often prefer what's familiar.
4. **Overly accommodating** – They say "yes" too often.
5. **Indecisive** – They can take too long to make a choice.
6. **Under the radar** – Their efforts may go unnoticed.
7. **Emotional bottling** – They suppress their own feelings.

8.
9. **Dependency risk** – Others can become too reliant on them.
10. **Martyr complex** – They take on too much to avoid burdening others.
11. **Overthinkers** – They can become paralyzed by analysis.
12. **Fear of letting others down** – Which can lead to burnout.
13. **Low self-promotion** – They rarely advocate for themselves.
14. **Tendency to hold grudges quietly** – Rather than confront.
15. **Struggle with saying "no"** – Even when overwhelmed.
16. **May enable underperformance** – By not holding others accountable.

Mild to Extreme: How Steadiness Shows Up

Mild Torch Leaders

These individuals are dependable, calm, and approachable, but don't seek to stand out. They tend to be quiet, reflecting their steady leadership style in one-on-one interactions. They prefer to support their team behind the scenes, providing stability and a sense of safety without being the center of attention.

Moderate Torch Leaders

Moderate Torch Leaders combine steadiness with a clear sense of reliability. They're patient and consistent, offering support to their team when needed, while still effectively managing group dynamics. They excel at creating a stable environment and building long-term trust without seeking recognition.

Extreme Torch Leaders

Extreme Torch Leaders can sometimes become overly passive or overshadowed by more dominant personalities. Their commitment to peace and stability may prevent them from asserting themselves when necessary, and they may struggle to take bold action in moments that require it. Their leadership is often quietly powerful but may go unnoticed unless actively recognized.

A Real Torch Leader: Mother Teresa

Anjezë Gonxhe Bojaxhiu, better known as Mother Teresa, embodied Torch Leadership through her unwavering commitment to serving the poor, sick, and forgotten. Working in the streets of

Calcutta, she didn't command authority or seek political power. Instead, her influence radiated from her steady compassion, quiet humility, and relentless presence among those in need. Even amid criticism and overwhelming poverty, she remained consistent, gentle, and faithful to her mission. Like a torch in the darkness, her leadership provided warmth, light, and hope—not through orders, but through example.

My Steady Coach

In high school, our soccer team went through a brutal slump. We dropped several matches in a row, and frustration was everywhere. Players were arguing during practice, the locker room grew quiet; a few teammates even started discussing quitting.

In the middle of all that chaos was Coach Smitka.

He wasn't the type to shout from the sidelines or deliver fiery locker-room speeches. Instead, he stayed calm, steady, and predictable. He reminded us that one bad week didn't define an entire season. On the field, he brought us back to the basic passing drills, ball control, and communication. And off the field, he kept a close eye on his players—checking in on those who looked discouraged, encouraging those who needed a boost, and reminding us of our strengths.

He kept asking the same grounding questions: *"What can we control on the field? How do we keep supporting each other as a team?"* He showed up the same way every day—steady, patient, and consistent.

We found our rhythm again—not because of a single dramatic moment or a half-time pep talk, but because Coach Smitka gave us something more valuable: stability. He was our torch. And when things felt shaky, his steady glow reminded us to keep moving forward together.

Another Example of a Torch Leader

Kirk is one of the most honest, sincere, and humble people I have ever met. If you have ever seen any of my dozens of videos on Leadership, Public Speaking, or Campfire Leadership on YouTube, the chances are that Kirk shot and edited the video. He said that he never wanted to be in front of the camera, but I knew he could have delivered the talk just as well, if not better, than I did. He would always encourage me to speak to the camera as if it were the group that I was standing in front of, not a camera. Not to use flowery language, but to convey it in a real and sincere manner. He always brought out the best in me with his encouragement and confidence. He utilized his strengths as a Torch Leader to make people feel good about themselves and inspired them to be the change they were trying to create.

As a side note, he later went on to create a series of his own videos. His attention to detail and ability to relate are unmatched by other video series I've seen. He is an excellent example of a Torch Leader stepping out from behind the camera to lead from the front when needed.

When Torch Leadership Shines Brightest

- **During uncertainty** – Their calm helps regulate group emotion.
- **In moments of conflict** – They listen first, speak second.
- **With new team members** – They're welcoming and patient.

- **When trust is fragile** – They help rebuild with consistency.
- **In long-term projects** – Their endurance keeps everyone on course.

How to Support a Torch Leader

Torch Leaders thrive when they:

- Feel safe and appreciated.
- Have time to process before making decisions.
- Are given consistency and clear expectations.
- Know that their efforts are seen and valued.

They need space to warm up to ideas, and they shine brightest when they're not being pressured to be someone else. If you've got a Torch on your team, you've got a treasure.

Balancing the Torch

While their steadiness is a strength, Torch Leaders must work to:

- Embrace conflict when necessary.
- Push past comfort zones.
- Speak up when their voice matters.
- Set boundaries to avoid burning out.
- Be open to change—even when it's uncomfortable.

Campfire Takeaway

Torch Leaders are the heartbeat of any team. They bring loyalty, warmth, and quiet strength. They may not chase the spotlight—but they keep the fire burning. In your journey toward becoming a Campfire Leader, learn from the Torch: stay steady, stay warm, and lead with calm courage.

Chapter 3 – The Spotlight Leader: Bold and Decisive

"Leaders should change the world and not just play the game."
—Rob Jackson

When the pressure is on and someone needs to make a tough call, all eyes shift to the **Spotlight Leader**. They don't shy away from the stage. They step into it.

In the DISC model, the Spotlight Leader represents the **Dominant (D)** personality type. These are your take-charge, high-intensity, action-oriented trailblazers. They are direct, assertive, and most of all—results-driven.

Spotlight Leaders want to get things done. Yesterday.

They don't wait for consensus. They seek clarity, cut through clutter, and create momentum. While others are still debating the problem, Spotlight Leaders have already proposed a solution, emailed, and made a follow-up call.

They thrive in uncertainty because it gives them a chance to lead. They are most comfortable when they're slightly uncomfortable. Challenge, change, and chaos are where they shine.

Strengths of a Spotlight Leader

1. **Decisive** – They make quick, confident decisions.
2. **Visionary** – They see the big picture and chase it boldly.
3. **Driven** – They have an unstoppable work ethic.
4. **Courageous** – They speak up, even when it's hard.

5. **Direct** – No sugarcoating, just clarity.
6. **Action-oriented** – They move fast and push others to do the same.
7. **Persistent** – They don't give up when things get tough.
8. **High standards** – They expect excellence from themselves and others.
9. **Confident** – Their belief in success is contagious.
10. **Goal-focused** – Everything is measured by outcomes.
11. **Independent** – They don't need micromanaging or hand-holding.
12. **Risk-takers** – They're willing to leap when others hesitate.
13. **Efficient** – They hate wasted time or resources.
14. **Problem-solvers** – They lean into challenges instead of avoiding them.
15. **Competitive** – They strive to be the best.

Opportunities for a Spotlight Leader

1. **Impatient** – They want results, now.
2. **Insensitive** – They bulldoze feelings without realizing it.
3. **Overconfident** – They may ignore input from others.
4. **Controlling** – Delegation doesn't come easily.
5. **Short-tempered** – Frustration flares quickly.
6. **Dismissive of detail** – They overlook the small stuff.
7. **Workaholic tendencies** – They can burn out or burn others out.
8. **Fear of failure** – They hide it under bravado.
9. **Low tolerance for indecision** – Slow thinkers frustrate them.
10. **Can be intimidating** – Their intensity can overwhelm softer personalities.

11. **Overly critical** – They focus on what's wrong, not what's working.
12. **Struggle with empathy** – They prioritize results over relationships.
13. **Hard to please** – Perfectionism sneaks in.
14. **Reluctant to ask for help** – They equate it with weakness.
15. **Struggle with vulnerability** – They fear appearing "soft."

Mild to Extreme: How Dominance Shows Up

Mild Spotlight Leaders

These leaders are naturally assertive and confident but don't always seek the spotlight. They are decisive in key moments but generally allow others to take charge when it's appropriate. They may lead with direction and clarity but are also open to input from others, balancing decisiveness with collaboration.

Moderate Spotlight Leaders

Moderate Spotlight Leaders excel in high-stakes situations, making clear and direct decisions that push the group forward. While they remain assertive and results-oriented, they understand when to let others take the lead. They balance their drive with an ability to listen and guide others toward solutions.

Extreme Spotlight Leaders

The spotlight thrives on attention and control, often dominating conversations and decisions. They may bulldoze over quieter team members and prioritize their own visibility and success over group collaboration. Their leadership can be intense, and their decisions may sometimes be more about demonstrating authority than reflecting careful thought.

A Real Spotlight Leader: Serena Williams

Serena Williams embodies Spotlight Leadership with her unmatched drive, dominance, and resilience. On the tennis court, her powerful presence demanded attention and set the tone for the sport. She raised standards, broke barriers, and inspired a generation with her fierce competitiveness and relentless pursuit of excellence. Beyond her victories, she used her platform to advocate for equality and perseverance. Like a spotlight cutting through darkness, Serena's leadership illuminated what was possible when confidence, talent, and determination converged.

The Mortgage Sales Manager Who Brought the Thunder

In my first year in the mortgage industry, I reported to a sales manager named Gary. Gary didn't just manage a team—he commanded it. You could hear his voice booming across the office, celebrating a closed loan or demanding an update on one that was stuck in underwriting. His energy filled the room, and when he walked into a client meeting, everyone knew he meant business.

Gary thrived on urgency. Quotas weren't just numbers to him; they were mountains to be climbed. His weekly pipeline reviews felt like being under a spotlight—you had to know your deals inside and out, and excuses weren't part of his vocabulary. At times, his intensity was exhausting, but it also raised our performance. He challenged every sales pitch, pushed us to build stronger referral relationships, and never let us coast when things got tough.

From Gary, I learned lessons that stayed with me: how to negotiate with confidence, how to stay composed when a deal hit roadblocks, and how to walk into a client's office like I belonged there. He wasn't warm and fuzzy, but he was always fair. His leadership took a team of average loan officers and turned us into a top-producing branch.

Gary was thunder—loud, relentless, and impossible to ignore. And in his storm, I learned how to sell with strength, resilience, and confidence.

An example of a not-so-great Spotlight Leader

I had the privilege of working for a man I'll call Rick. I only call it a privilege because I learned how not to treat people. He is an example of an Extreme Spotlight. He was a very driven Entrepreneur that I worked for before starting my own company. He treated me and his other employees as if we were children. He constantly berated everyone whenever he didn't like what we did. Then he would use the person as a negative example, allowing everyone to see their mistake and how Rick corrected them, ultimately saving the world from a near-earth-ending blunder. He would ask your opinion only to validate a decision he had already made or tell you that you were wrong if you had an idea different than his. He taught me how not to treat people. Where he used intimidation, I learned to use persuasion and patience. Not everyone you meet is a good example of the person you want to be, but Rick was an example of what you may not want to be. But both are important to see when you're trying to develop into a Campfire Leader.

When Spotlight Leadership Shines Brightest

- **During crises** – They act fast and lead the charge.
- **When a decision must be made** – They don't stall or shy away.
- **When goals need to be hit** – They align everyone on the mission.
- **In competitive environments** – Their edge becomes an asset.
- **With strong-willed teams** – They match energy with energy.

How to Support a Spotlight Leader

They thrive when:

- You get to the point—fast.
- You respect their time.
- You don't take their bluntness personally.
- You bring solutions, not just problems.
- You allow them to lead—but challenge them with honesty.

Don't expect handholding. Do expect intensity. If you're on their team, be ready to run.

Balancing the Spotlight

To grow, Spotlight Leaders must:

- Listen actively—not just hear, but understand.
- Practice empathy, especially with softer personalities.
- Slow down and celebrate small wins.
- Learn to delegate and develop others.
- Recognize that relationships drive results too.

Campfire Takeaway

Spotlight Leaders are bold, brilliant, and built for action. They move things forward and challenge others to rise. But power without presence can turn into pressure. A Campfire Leader learns to balance intensity with inspiration.

Lead with fire, not fury.

Chapter 4 – The Disco Light Leader (The Influential Style)

"Leadership is not about being in the spotlight; it's about knowing when to shine and when to let others shine."
— Rob Jackson

Some leaders enter a room, and everything changes. The smiles increase. The energy rises. That's the Disco Light Leader in action—a natural-born influencer whose charisma can light up even the dullest boardroom.

Disco Light Leaders are easy to spot—not because they're loud (though sometimes they are)—but because they're magnetic. They want to connect. They want to be heard. And most of all, they want to motivate themselves. In the DISC model, these leaders closely align with the Influence (I) style, characterized by enthusiasm, persuasion, relational skills, and a people-focused approach. Imagine a disco ball spinning in the center of the dance floor, capturing the attention of everyone as it reflects light in every direction. It's never static. It moves. It engages. It dazzles. So does the Disco Light Leader.

These leaders operate with emotion and expression. You'll find them giving high-fives in the hallway, leading the company cheer, or energizing a team meeting with jokes, metaphors, and a sense of momentum. Where others might hesitate, the Disco Light Leader dives in headfirst, often relying on charm and people skills to achieve their vision.

Traits and Behaviors of a Disco Light Leader

- Highly expressive and animated
- Strong verbal communication and storytelling abilities

- Motivated by praise, recognition, and group collaboration
- Frequently seen rallying others or persuading them into action
- Seeks enthusiastic environments with a lot of interpersonal energy
- Tends to avoid conflict and detail-heavy tasks

Disco Light Leaders are particularly effective in high-morale situations or when rallying support is needed to launch a new product. Starting a grassroots campaign? Building buzz around a major initiative? Let the Disco Light take the mic. They'll have the crowd standing on chairs, metaphorically (and sometimes literally).

Strengths of a Disco Light Leader

1. Charismatic – They draw people in with their energy and enthusiasm.
2. Optimistic – They bring a positive outlook, even in challenging situations.
3. Engaging – They make people feel heard and understood.
4. Persuasive – They can motivate others to take action and embrace new ideas.
5. Energetic – They inject high energy into meetings and interactions.
6. Inspiring – They make others believe they can achieve great things.
7. Adaptable – They easily adjust to changing environments and people.
8. Relational – They build strong connections with others.
9. Expressive – They convey ideas and emotions in a dynamic, impactful way.
10. Social – They thrive in interactive, group-focused settings.

11. Fun-loving – They make work enjoyable, fostering a sense of camaraderie.
12. Motivational – They encourage others to perform at their best.
13. Collaborative – They work well in teams and energize group dynamics.
14. Visionary – They can see potential and inspire others to follow that vision.
15. Authentic – Their genuine approach builds trust and rapport.

Opportunities for a Disco Light Leader

1. Overpromising – They may commit to more than they can deliver in the heat of excitement.
2. Impulsive – Their enthusiasm can sometimes lead to hasty decisions.
3. Easily Distracted – They can lose focus on the task at hand due to their eagerness to engage.
4. Avoids Conflict – They may steer clear of difficult conversations, leaving issues unresolved.
5. Overly Emotional – Their expressive nature can sometimes overshadow rational thinking.
6. Lacks Attention to Detail – They may overlook finer details while focusing on the big picture.
7. Seek Approval – Their desire for validation can sometimes influence their decisions.
8. Disorganized – They might struggle with managing logistics or structured planning.
9. Inconsistent – Their energy levels can vary, affecting team dynamics.
10. Struggles with Follow-Through – They may get distracted before completing tasks.

11. Can Be Overbearing – Their drive to inspire can come across as too intense for some.
12. Discomfort with Criticism – They may have a hard time accepting negative feedback.
13. Reluctance to Set Boundaries – They may let their enthusiasm interfere with maintaining professional limits.
14. May Depend on Charm – Their natural charisma can sometimes substitute for substance.
15. Overextends – Their eagerness to help everyone can lead to burnout.

Mild to Extreme: How Influence Shows Up

Mild Disco Light Leaders
These individuals tend to be warm, conversational, and collaborative but don't seek the spotlight. They prefer one-on-one influence over crowd appeal and may work behind the scenes, building support through personal connections.

Moderate Disco Light Leaders
This group balances performance and purpose. They use their voice to encourage others but maintain some structure and boundaries. They understand when to inspire and when to step back.

Extreme Disco Light Leaders
The spotlight becomes oxygen. These leaders often dominate conversations, may overshadow quieter team members, and can fall into a "show mode." Their decisions may be influenced more by applause than by substance.

A Real Disco Light Leader: Richard Branson

Richard Branson, founder of the Virgin Group, is a true example of Disco Light Leadership in the business world. From airlines to record labels to space exploration, Branson has built an empire not just through strategy, but through charisma, optimism, and a magnetic personality. He has a way of drawing people in, whether they're employees, customers, or the media.

What makes Branson stand out is that his leadership never feels distant or rigid. He's the kind of leader who will show up to a product launch in costume or literally risk embarrassment to prove he believes in an idea. He doesn't rely on authority or hierarchy—he relies on connection. His energy communicates, *"If I can dream big, so can you."*

Inside his companies, Branson is known for being approachable and encouraging. He remembers names, values people's ideas, and takes the time to listen. Employees often describe him as someone who creates an atmosphere of fun and possibility, even when the challenges are serious. Customers, too, feel that Virgin isn't just selling them a product, but inviting them into an experience.

That's the power of a Disco Light Leader. The influence spreads in all directions, bouncing off every interaction and leaving people feeling inspired, energized, and valued. Branson's light doesn't just illuminate his own success—it reflects on those around him, reminding them of their own potential. His story proves that in business, the spark of human connection can be just as powerful as a spreadsheet or strategy.

The Speaker Who Lit Up the Room

A few years ago, I worked with a keynote speaker named Marcus. Marcus was pure Disco Light. He didn't just step on stage—he *exploded* onto it. The music, the smile, the energy—he had audiences leaning forward before he said a single word. He told stories that made people laugh, cry, and jump to their feet in standing ovations.

But Marcus had a blind spot. Behind the scenes, he avoided the details. He'd show up late to rehearsals, skim through contracts, and sometimes deliver talks that strayed from the client's theme. One time, he improvised so much at a leadership conference that he skipped half the agreed-upon content. The audience loved him, but the event planner did not. Trust wobbled.

Afterward, I asked him a simple question: *"Do you want to be remembered as inspiring, or as entertaining?"* He went quiet for the first time all week. That moment stuck.

Marcus didn't dim his light—he learned to direct it. He started working closely with detail-oriented partners who helped him prepare and keep promises. He still lit up every stage, but now his influence lasted long after the applause faded. Marcus remained a Disco Light Leader—but he learned how to shine responsibly.

What Campfire Leaders Can Learn from Disco Light Leaders

A Campfire Leader understands the power of presence, but also the responsibility of it. Influence without responsibility is just noise.

The Disco Light Leader teaches us that leadership should have rhythm, emotion, and personality. People need to feel *seen*, and no one makes people feel seen like the Disco Light Leader. But that spotlight must eventually shift to others.

When balanced, the Disco Light Leader is a force for good—igniting morale, championing people, and rallying movements. When imbalanced, they risk burning out their team with enthusiasm that lacks execution.

Campfire Takeaway

A Campfire Leader borrows the warmth and connectivity of the Disco Light—but uses it to light the path, not blind the followers.

Chapter 5 – The Lighthouse Leader (The Conscientious Style)

"Lighthouse Leaders don't chase storms; they prepare others for them." — Rob Jackson

Every organization needs someone who sees the storm before anyone else. Someone who isn't loud, flashy, or desperate for attention—but who shows up, steady and sharp, when others are spinning in chaos. That's the Lighthouse Leader.

Lighthouse Leaders are the most measured and principle-driven of all leadership styles. In the DISC model, they reflect the *C* type: conscientious, detail-oriented, analytical, and dependable. While others are rushing in to lead the charge or ignite energy, the Lighthouse Leader is assessing risk, cross-checking assumptions, and quietly guiding the ship to safety. They may not always be seen, but when things get murky, everyone looks for the lighthouse.

Lighthouse Leaders are logic-based leaders. They build trust not through charisma or command, but through competence and expertise.
Their strength lies in their ability to stay calm, think critically, and act precisely. When they speak, it carries weight—because they've done the homework.

Traits and Behaviors of a Lighthouse Leader

- Values logic, precision, and accuracy
- Leads through process, structure, and planning
- Avoids unnecessary risks; favors data-driven decisions
- Is cautious with praise but sincere when given

- Often introverted or reflective in group settings
- Seeks stability, clarity, and fairness

Lighthouse Leaders don't dominate the spotlight, but they quietly influence outcomes through careful strategy. They are the system builders and quality controllers of leadership. In moments of pressure, their calm demeanor is a welcome counterbalance to more reactive styles.

Strengths of a Lighthouse Leader

1. Organized – They plan meticulously, ensuring that every detail is accounted for.
2. Calm – They remain steady in high-pressure situations, providing a sense of stability.
3. Critical Thinker – They analyze situations from all angles before making decisions.
4. Consistent – They can be relied upon to make fair, predictable decisions.
5. Fair – They approach situations with a sense of impartiality and equity.
6. Detail-Oriented – They focus on the small, important details that others may overlook.
7. Reliable – Others can trust that they will uphold their responsibilities and commitments.
8. Thoughtful – They consider all perspectives before taking action.
9. Strategic – They always have a long-term plan in mind, balancing risk and reward.
10. Resourceful – They are skilled at finding solutions in challenging situations.
11. Responsible – They take ownership of their actions and decisions.

12. Patient – They allow time for thoughtful reflection and careful planning.
13. Knowledgeable – Their expertise makes them a go-to resource in times of uncertainty.
14. Grounded – They maintain a clear and steady presence, no matter what happens.
15. Wise – Their approach to leadership is shaped by experience and careful observation.

Opportunities for a Lighthouse Leader

1. Perfectionistic – They may struggle with accepting anything less than flawless results.
2. Risk-Averse – Their caution may lead them to avoid necessary risks.
3. Over-Analytical – They may take too long to make decisions, delaying progress.
4. Detached – Their focus on logic may make them appear distant or unapproachable.
5. Rigid – They may resist change or unconventional approaches.
6. Hesitant to Delegate – They can be reluctant to trust others with important tasks.
7. Overly Cautious – Their careful nature can sometimes prevent them from taking bold actions.
8. Indecisive – They may struggle to make quick decisions in high-pressure moments.
9. Overburdened – They may take on too much responsibility, fearing that others won't meet their standards.

10. Insensitive – Their focus on facts and processes can make them seem cold or unfeeling.
11. Pessimistic – Their strategic foresight may make them overly cautious, even in situations that could benefit from optimism.
12. Detached from Emotions – They may not always recognize or address emotional undercurrents in the team.
13. Tends to Micromanage – Their need for control can lead them to micromanage team members.
14. Overthinks – They may become paralyzed by their own thought processes, struggling to move forward.
15. Can Be Overly Critical – They may focus too much on what's wrong, rather than celebrating what's working.

Mild to Extreme: How Conscientiousness Shows Up

Mild Lighthouse Leaders

Mild C-style leaders are thoughtful and balanced. They uphold standards but are open to input and feedback. They make excellent mediators or quality mentors who favor calm influence.

Moderate Lighthouse Leaders

These leaders strike a balance between analysis and action. They plan before moving and are most effective in high-responsibility roles where their thoroughness can shine.

Extreme Lighthouse Leaders

An extreme C-type can fall into analysis paralysis. They delay decisions, nitpick performance, and become inflexible under pressure. The need for perfection may trump progress, stalling momentum.

A Real Lighthouse Leader: Captain "Sully" Sullenberger

Chesley "Sully" Sullenberger became a household name after January 15, 2009—the day he embodied Lighthouse Leadership in its purest form. Shortly after takeoff from LaGuardia Airport, US Airways Flight 1549 struck a flock of geese, knocking out both engines. With only seconds to act, and the lives of 155 people in his hands, Sully remained calm. He evaluated the situation, communicated clearly with air traffic control, and made a decision that defied conventional procedure: landing an Airbus A320 on the Hudson River.

What made Sully's leadership extraordinary wasn't just the outcome—it was the steadiness behind it. Years of preparation, discipline, and attention to detail shaped that moment. He wasn't flashy or dramatic. He didn't grand stand. He simply did what needed to be done, with unwavering focus and composure, even as chaos unfolded around him. His co-pilot later recalled how Sully's calm instructions steadied the cockpit and kept panic from taking over.

Sully didn't seek the spotlight or applause. In fact, when the media hailed him as a hero, he humbly redirected the credit to his crew, the flight attendants, and the first responders who assisted passengers on the river. That humility is the hallmark of Lighthouse Leadership—guidance without ego, service without demand for recognition.

Like a lighthouse standing firm against crashing waves, Sully's leadership provided clarity, stability, and direction in the middle of a storm. He reminded the world that real leadership isn't measured in titles or charisma—it's proven in critical moments when others are looking for someone steady enough to trust.

The "Miracle on the Hudson" wasn't just a story of survival—it was a testament to what Lighthouse Leadership looks like when everything is on the line: prepared, principled, calm, and unshakably dependable.

Another Real Lighthouse Leader: Warren Buffett

Warren Buffett, the legendary investor and CEO of Berkshire Hathaway, is one of the clearest examples of Lighthouse Leadership in the business world. For decades, he has guided investors, employees, and even other CEOs with a calm, principled approach that contrasts sharply with the high-stakes, adrenaline-fueled culture of Wall Street.

Buffett doesn't chase trends or quick wins. His decisions are grounded in preparation, patience, and timeless principles. He communicates with striking clarity—his annual shareholder letters cut through noise and complexity, providing steadiness and reassurance.

When markets crumble, Buffett's voice has often steadied entire industries. During the 2008 financial crisis, for example, his decision to invest in firms like Goldman Sachs wasn't just a business move—it was a signal to the world that panic wasn't the answer. His lighthouse-like steadiness has made him a beacon not only for investors but for leaders seeking calm in turbulence.

Buffett proves that leadership doesn't always need charisma or fanfare. Sometimes, the truest power comes from being the consistent light that helps others navigate through storms.

The Engineer Who Always Saw It Coming

At a manufacturing company where I consulted, there was an engineer named Daniel who embodied Lighthouse Leadership. He wasn't the one presenting flashy slides in meetings or tossing around bold predictions. While others brainstormed marketing campaigns and new product launches, Daniel was running simulations, reviewing safety data, and quietly drafting backup plans.

Some colleagues teased him for being overly cautious. "Daniel always has a worst-case scenario," they'd laugh. And most of the time, his careful notes went unnoticed.

Until the day a critical machine on the factory floor failed. Production halted, managers scrambled, and panic spread. That's when Daniel calmly walked to his desk, pulled out a thick binder, and said, *"Here's the plan we talked about six months ago, if this ever happened."*

Because of his preparation, the team was back online within days instead of weeks. His quiet diligence had saved the company time, money, and credibility with their clients.

Daniel didn't brag. He didn't need to. His steady presence and foresight spoke for him. A lighthouse doesn't rush to the rescue—it simply stands prepared, shining the light that guides others through the storm.

What Campfire Leaders Can Learn from Lighthouse Leaders

Lighthouse Leaders demonstrate that leadership isn't always about volume—it's about vision and vigilance.

A Campfire Leader embraces the Lighthouse's precision, calm, and long-range thinking. They respect the importance of detail, process, and preparation, especially when the fire needs to be tended to for the long haul.

Lighthouse Leaders may not crave the front line, but they create the safety rails that keep the team on course. They remind us that behind every inspiring story or rousing speech is someone who made sure the numbers lined up, the plan made sense, and the risks were minimized.

Campfire Takeaway

In the campfire, we need warmth—but we also need structure. A Campfire Leader borrows the integrity and intentionality of the Lighthouse Leader to ensure the flame keeps burning strong.

Chapter 6 – Mental Wellbeing: Protecting the Flame Within

"Health is a state of complete physical, mental, and social well-being and not merely the absence of disease or infirmity."
—Heave

You might be asking yourselves why I am including Mental Wellbeing in a Leadership book. I think that Mental well-being is one of the most overlooked components of leadership—and yet, it's the one thing that holds everything else together.

It wasn't until the mid-19th century that mental health was even acknowledged as a legitimate concern. William Sweetser introduced the concept of "mental hygiene," recognizing that just like physical health, the mind needs regular care and attention. And yet today, even with all our progress, stigma still surrounds mental health—especially in the workplace.

Why? Because talking about burnout, anxiety, or overwhelm can still be misread as weakness. But the truth is this: **mental wellbeing is not a luxury—it's a leadership necessity.**

Workplace Realities: When the Mind Suffers

confidence-shattering experiences are often born in the workplace. An off-hand comment, a toxic boss, a relentless workload—these things chip away at self-worth. People begin to feel *worthless*. When that happens, performance suffers, motivation evaporates, and the spiral begins.

Even worse? When someone tries to talk about it, they're told to "tough it out" or "stop complaining." This is especially common in fast-paced work environments, where silence is mistaken for strength.

But leadership—*real* leadership—demands we do better. We need to create spaces where people feel safe being human.

The Definition That Matters

Mental well-being is more than just the absence of depression or anxiety. It's about feeling emotionally safe, stable, and satisfied. It's the ability to regulate emotions, manage stress, connect with others, and adapt to change.

When someone feels emotionally safe, they can tap into their full potential. But when they're mentally drained? No amount of caffeine, deadlines, or pep talks can compensate for the crash that's coming.

The environment plays a critical role here. A toxic environment poisons the mind. A positive one helps it grow.

Pressure: Motivation or Mayhem?

There's a thin line between *productive pressure* and *destructive stress*.

The best leaders know how to challenge their people without crushing them. They assign tasks based on capability—not just urgency. They stretch people without snapping them.

When pressure turns into chronic stress, mental and physical health suffer. Sleep deprivation creeps in. Mistakes increase.

Morale plummets. Soon, even the most competent people begin to question their worth.

A Campfire Leader always asks themselves: *Are my expectations building my team—or breaking them?*

Error Is Part of Life

Mistakes don't always come from incompetence. Often, they come from exhaustion.

Sleep-deprived brains misfire. Overloaded minds miss details. And people under chronic stress develop *learned helplessness*—a belief that nothing they do will be enough.

A bad leader sees an error and berates the employee, as seen in my earlier example with Rick.

A Campfire Leader sees the mistake and asks, *what support is missing?*

Campfire Leaders help people understand that mistakes are part of growth. They don't pretend to be perfect—and they don't expect perfection in others.

Mental Health = Physical Health

There's a saying:

"Sickness of the mind becomes sickness of the body."

This isn't just poetic—it's proven. Chronic stress is linked to everything from heart disease to autoimmune disorders. Anxiety impacts digestion, memory, and focus. Depression can make a physically healthy person bedridden.

Conversely, when someone is mentally well, their immune system improves, their energy returns, and their resilience strengthens. One fuels the other. Great leaders protect both.

Incompetent Leadership Is a Health Risk

Stats don't lie: People under toxic leadership are more likely to report symptoms of anxiety, depression, and burnout.

Why? Because bad leaders:

- Blame others without taking responsibility.
- Dismiss concerns.
- Micromanage.
- Prioritize output over people.

Incompetent leaders fail to recognize their own faults. And when leaders never self-reflect, their employees suffer. That's not just bad management—it's a moral failure.

Campfire Leaders, on the other hand, lead with self-awareness. They know their ripple effects matter. And they use that influence to create healthier teams.

The Human Cost of Production

Economics teaches us that the cost of a product is the sum of the resources used to make it. But in human terms, what's the **cost** of production?

Too often, the answer is: **burnout.**

If a successful project leaves a trail of exhausted and emotionally wrecked employees in its wake, can it truly be called a success?

Campfire Leaders know the answer is no.

Working to Death

In many industries, particularly healthcare and technology, burnout has reached epidemic proportions. Overwork has become a badge of honor—and people are literally working themselves to death.

This is not leadership. This is a failure of leadership.

Great leaders:

- Set boundaries.
- Model balance.
- Encourage recovery.
- Normalize saying "I need help."

No task is worth sacrificing a human being's mental health.

How to Care for Mental Well-being on Your Team

Be Considerate

See your team members as whole individuals, not just job titles. Know what's happening in their lives. Show up with empathy, not just expectations.

Be Respectful

Respect isn't just about tone. It's about how you handle mistakes. How do you give feedback? How do you protect people's dignity? Respect is the soil where trust grows.

Workplace Politics & Psychological Safety

Workplace politics can be toxic. Gossip, favoritism, and hidden agendas—all these erode mental well-being.

A Campfire Leader addresses this head-on. They eliminate silos. They name dysfunctions. They create psychological safety by saying, 'Here, we don't play games.' *We grow together.*

Good Mental Health Is Good Business

Happy teams produce better results. Period.

- They're more creative.
- They collaborate more.
- They stay longer.
- They bring positive energy to clients.

Campfire Leaders don't see mental wellness as a "soft" issue. They see it as a **strategic advantage**.

"The purpose of training is to tighten the slack, toughen the body, and polish the spirit."
—Morihei Ueshiba

Training isn't just about technical skills. It's about *resilience*. And resilience is born when leaders make mental well-being a daily practice—not just a one-time pep talk.

Campfire Takeaway

The fire you're building will only last if you protect its fuel. People can't burn bright if they're burning out.

Mental well-being is not a footnote in leadership. It's the foundation. And if you want your people to rise, you must first give them room to breathe.

The best leaders don't just spark success, they sustain it. And they do it by caring for the minds and hearts that make the mission possible.

Chapter 7 – Easy to Trust: Building the Bridge That Lasts

"Trust is the highest form of human motivation. It brings out the very best in people."
—Stephen R. Covey

Trust is a delicate thing. It's hard to build, easy to break, and nearly impossible to repair once it's shattered. We all know that gut-clenching feeling of being burned. Whether it occurred in our childhood, early career, or just last week, trust violations leave lasting marks.

In life, we might give people the benefit of the doubt. But in the workplace? We're more guarded. Why? Here, trust isn't just emotional; it's **professional**. It affects performance, collaboration, creativity, and results.

And when trust is absent, everything suffers.

The Leadership Trust Crisis

Let's be honest—many employees don't trust their leaders. And sometimes, leaders don't trust their teams either.

What causes that breakdown?

- Poor communication
- Inconsistent follow-through
- Fear-based leadership
- A lack of approachability

Trust isn't earned by title—it's earned by behavior. Campfire Leaders don't assume they're trusted just because they're in charge. They **work** for it.

Why Trust = Performance

Workplace trust isn't just nice to have—it's a performance multiplier.

When employees trust their leaders, they:

- Take ownership
- Admit mistakes early
- Share ideas freely
- Collaborate instead of competing
- Work harder because they care—not because they're scared

When they **don't** trust leadership, the opposite happens:

- Silence replaces feedback
- Innovation dies
- Morale plummets
- Turnover rises

Trust is the oil in the engine. Without it, everything grinds.

The Two Biggest Trust Killers

If your employees don't trust you, it often boils down to one (or both) of the following:

1. **They are afraid of you.**
2. **You are unapproachable.**

It's that simple—and that devastating. A Campfire Leader breaks both barriers. They're strong, but not scary. Supportive, but not passive.

How to Become a Trustworthy Leader

So, how do you become the kind of leader others feel safe following?

Let's break it down.

1. Keep Your Behavior in Check 24/7

You are being watched—not in a creepy way, but in a *leadership-is-a-lighthouse* kind of way. Your tone, body language, and reactions set the emotional thermostat for your team.

Campfire Leaders lead with self-awareness. They reflect often and ask:

- *Did I handle that with grace?*
- *Did I overreact or under-respond?*
- *Did I model the behavior I want to see?*

The behavior of a leader ripples across the room. Keep your waves positive.

2. Stay Flexible, Not Fragile

Adaptability is a leadership superpower. The world changes fast. Plans go sideways. People need different things.

A rigid leader loses relevance. A flexible leader earns trust by saying, *Let's find a better way together.*

Campfire Leaders embrace uncertainty, adjust when needed, and never punish people for speaking up about change.

3. Tell It Like It Is—But with Kindness

Transparency matters. People respect honest leaders. But too often, leaders confuse "honesty" with "harshness."

Here's the truth: **You can be direct without being demeaning.**

Campfire Leaders give feedback with clarity and care. They correct without crushing. They hold high standards *and* high respect.

4. Remember: People Don't Quit Jobs, They Quit Bad Leaders

A fancy title doesn't keep good talent. Good treatment does.

Employees leave when:

- They're micromanaged
- They feel belittled
- They're afraid to speak up
- Their effort goes unrecognized

Leaders with superiority complexes can quickly drain morale. Campfire Leaders don't remind people of their title—they remind people of their **worth**.

5. Confide—Don't Explode

Leadership is hard. The pressure is real. But pressure doesn't excuse poor behavior.

When you're overwhelmed, please don't take it out on your team. Find a trusted peer, mentor, or friend. Vent. Process. Reset.

A Campfire Leader manages emotion responsibly. They don't dump stress on their people. They channel it into strategy.

6. Practice Action-Based Trust

Don't tell your team to trust you. **Show them** they can.

That means:

- Following through on promises
- Owning mistakes
- Giving credit where it's due

- Being consistent—not moody

Your words don't build trust. Your *pattern of behavior* does.

7. Encourage Autonomy, Not Dependency

It's easy to become a team hero. Answer every question. Solve every problem. Be the go-to fixer.

But Campfire Leaders know that real trust is built when you say, *"I trust you to figure this out."*

Empower your team to think, decide, and lead—even when you're not in the room.

8. Talk About the Tough Stuff

Trust grows in truth.

If you've made mistakes in the past as a leader, say so. If you're working on a behavior, let your team know. Vulnerability—when balanced with strength—builds massive trust.

Campfire Leaders own their humanity. And in doing so, they permit others to do the same.

Are Your Employees Happy with You?

Statistics say only 45% of employees feel appreciated at work. That means **more than half don't.**

What does that say about leadership?

Campfire Leaders fix this by being intentional:

- Recognize good work out loud
- Celebrate small wins
- Ask how people are doing—and mean it

Trust is built in moments, not meetings.

Final Sparks of Wisdom

Trust is not a luxury of leadership; it's a **requirement**. Without it, your culture crumbles. With it, your team thrives.

Campfire Leaders:

- Are strong without being scary
- Are honest without being harsh
- Are open without being weak

They know that trust isn't given by default—it's **earned by design**.

In the next chapter, we'll look at how to balance power and authority—a natural next step in building a team that follows you not just because they have to, but because they want to.

Chapter 8 – Balancing Power and Authority

"Authority and power do not hold the ability to change a person. They merely reveal their true intentions."
—Rob Jackson

Power. It's one of the most dangerous tools a leader can wield—and one of the most transformative.

We've all seen what happens when someone "gets a little power." Their tone shifts. Their humility shrinks. Their ego inflates like a balloon on a hot day.

But here's the truth: **Power doesn't change a person. It reveals who they already were.** That's why understanding how to use it—wisely and responsibly—is one of the most essential skills of a Campfire Leader.

Power: A Double-Edged Torch

Power is like fire. It can light the way or burn everything down.

The moment someone is given power; they face a choice:

- Use it as a tool to elevate others
- Or wield it as a weapon to control

Sadly, too many leaders fall into the second camp. They confuse being **in charge** with being **in control.** A Campfire Leader knows the difference—and they never mistake fear for respect.

Types pf Power: The Six Faces of Influence

Years ago, social psychologists **John French and Bertram Raven** categorized power into six types. These categories are just as relevant today—and knowing which one you lean into is crucial.

Let's break them down with real-world clarity:

1. Legitimate Power

This is the power that comes with a title. Manager. Supervisor. Director. CEO.

It's granted by the organization and tied to your role—not your personality.

The catch? Once you lose the title, you lose the influence… unless you've built more than a nameplate.

Campfire Leaders earn trust that outlasts the org chart. Their impact isn't linked to their label—it's rooted in their values.

2. Reward Power

You give praise, bonuses, promotions, and perks. This power motivates—when used well.

But beware:
If you only reward people who flatter you or say yes to everything, you're building a house of cards. Rewards without fairness create resentment.

Campfire Leaders use reward power to celebrate growth, not manipulate behavior.

3. Coercive Power

This is the power of punishment. Threats. Demotions. Harsh criticism. Fear.

It works... briefly. But the cost? High turnover, disengagement, and a culture of silence.

Campfire Leaders never rule through fear. They understand that fear shuts down creativity, trust, and courage.

4. Expert Power

This is the power that comes from competence. You've been there, done it. People trust your judgment because you've earned it.

Campfire Leaders use expert power to teach, guide, and mentor—not to show off.

5. Reverent Power

This is the power of charisma, character, and connection. People follow you because they **want to**, not because they must.

Think: the leader everyone wants to work with again.

Campfire Leaders build referent power by showing integrity, empathy, and humility.

6. Informational Power

This one was added later—it's the power of access. You have the insights others need.

Used poorly? It becomes gatekeeping.
Used well? It becomes empowerment.

Campfire Leaders share knowledge freely, helping others make better decisions.

Authority vs. Power: Know the Difference

Let's clear this up:

- **Power** is the ability to influence.
- **Authority** is the permission to lead.

You can have power without authority. You can have authority without power. But the most effective leaders **balance both**.

Campfire Leaders don't wait for permission to make an impact—but they respect the responsibility that comes with their position.

Max Weber's 3 Types of Authority

Sociologist **Max Weber** defined three classic kinds of authority. Understanding these helps leaders self-assess and grow. We can also learn from the mistakes each of these types of personalities is prone to making.

1. Charismatic Authority

Magnetic leadership through personality, passion, and inspiration.

Examples:

- **Startup Founder's Rally Cry** – A visionary founder inspires their small team to work nights and weekends because they can see the dream so vividly. People follow because they believe in *them* as much as in the idea.
- **Coach with a Cause** – A high school coach fires up the team with passionate speeches, making players believe they can beat impossible odds—and sometimes, they do.
- **Influential Keynote Speaker** – A leader steps on stage and captivates the entire room, leaving everyone ready to act on their message. The movement grows because of their personal appeal.

Pitfalls:

- Can become a **personality cult** where decisions rely more on the leader's charm than on sound reasoning.
- Risk of **burnout** if the leader's personal energy is the only thing driving momentum.
- If the leader leaves, the movement may **collapse** because it's not built on systems or shared ownership.

2. Legal-Rational Authority

Grounded in structure, policies, and fair process.

Examples:

- **Corporate Compliance Officer** – Ensures safety procedures are followed, not to stifle creativity, but to keep everyone safe and within the law.
- **Project Manager with Clear SOPs** – Uses well-documented workflows so any team member can jump in and contribute without chaos.
- **Judge in a Courtroom** – Holds authority because of established law and process, ensuring each case is heard fairly and consistently.

Pitfalls:

- Can become **bureaucratic gridlock**, where red tape slows progress unnecessarily.
- Employees may feel **like numbers**, losing motivation because everything feels impersonal.
- Strict adherence to rules may **stifle innovation** when people fear breaking protocol to try something new.

3. Traditional Authority

Rooted in "the way we've always done it."

Examples:

- **Family Business Patriarch** – A third-generation leader who makes key decisions because that's how the family business has always been run.
- **Religious or Cultural Leader** – A rabbi, priest, or elder whose authority comes from tradition and the respect their role has carried for centuries.
- **Organizational Rituals** – Annual company celebrations or ceremonies that are led by the longest-tenured employees because it's "their role."

Pitfalls:

- Can resist **necessary change**, holding the organization back in outdated ways.
- May unintentionally **exclude newcomers** or fresh ideas because "they haven't earned it yet."
- Over-reliance on tradition can lead to **complacency**, ignoring new challenges or opportunities.

The Danger of Imbalance

Many leaders start with good intentions but fall into one of these traps:

- They gain legitimate authority but crave referent power—so they fake charisma.

- They wield coercive power when expert power would've built more trust.
- They use authority as a crutch instead of developing real leadership presence.

Balance matters.

How Campfire Leaders Keep Power in Check

Here's how Campfire Leaders carry the torch without letting it burn others:

1. They Don't Lose Direction

Power can make you forget your purpose. Stay mission-focused. Don't let the title distract you from the reason you're leading in the first place.

2. They Invite Freedom of Choice

Great leaders don't hoard decisions. They empower others to act, think, and contribute.

3. They Maintain Healthy Boundaries

You can be friendly—but you're still the leader. Campfire Leaders are warm without becoming doormats.

4. They Practice Humility

You're never too high up to be wrong—or to learn. Campfire Leaders stay grounded and real.

5. They Ask for Suggestions

Who is the most intelligent person in the room? Often, it's not the one talking the most. Campfire Leaders seek feedback and value team input.

6. They Are Firm—but Thoughtful

Authority isn't a license to bulldoze. Campfire Leaders correct in private, praise in public, and lead with intention—not impulse.

Influence Is the True Legacy

Ultimately, your title will change. Your team may turn over. But the influence you leave behind?

That's what lasts.

Campfire Leaders influence by:

- Modeling the behaviors they expect
- Creating space for others to grow
- Sharing power, not clinging to it
- Leading in a way that others want to follow, even in their absence

Power and authority will open doors. Influence is what keeps them open.

In the next chapter, we'll explore the deeper art of **influencing future leaders**—because Campfire Leadership doesn't stop with you. It multiplies through others.

Chapter 9 – Influencing Future Leaders

"Leadership is about making sure you lead others properly in your presence. Influence, on the other hand, is the ability to guide others in your absence."
—Rob Jackson

Have you ever noticed how powerful influence can be—when it's used for good?

Unlike power, which pushes people, or authority, which gives permission, **influence pulls people in**. It inspires change without shouting. It leads without demanding. It nudges without force.

A Campfire Leader doesn't just lead—they influence. They don't just tell people where to go—they show them how to walk the path and then trust them to take it. They light the way, then step aside so others can shine.

Why Influence Matters More Than Ever

In today's workplace, people don't follow titles. They follow trust. They follow consistency. They follow **influence**.

It's the subtle difference between a manager and a mentor… between being obeyed and being believed.

Power controls.
Influence inspires.

In college, I had a soccer coach who rarely yelled. While other coaches barked orders from the sidelines, Coach Karns asked questions. *"What did you see on that play?"* or *"How would you adjust?"* He didn't need to throw his weight around—we already knew he was the coach.

But because he listened, I trusted him. I ran harder, pushed further, and respected his feedback because it felt like he was invested in *me*, not just the scoreboard. He influenced me to give my best—not through fear, but through trust.

The Double-Edged Nature of Influence

Just like power, influence can be used for good or ill.

Think of **peer pressure.** That's influence. Imagine a toxic workplace culture that fosters gossip rather than gratitude. That's an influence too.

But think of the coworker who models healthy boundaries, or the leader who lifts others in every meeting—they're quietly transforming the team, one moment at a time.

The best kind of influence is the one that leaves people better than it found them.

I once worked on a team where the culture leaned negative. A few coworkers loved to huddle in the break room and vent about everything—leadership, deadlines, clients. At first, it felt good to be included. Their influence made me feel like I belonged. However, I noticed something: the more time I spent in those conversations, the more drained I felt as I walked back to my desk. My attitude shifted, and not for the better.

Around that same time, there was another teammate—Angela. She never got caught up in the gossip. She worked hard, kept healthy boundaries, and always found a way to highlight what was working instead of what was broken. She didn't preach; she just modeled it. And little by little, her influence rubbed off on me. I found myself wanting to spend more time around her than in the negativity of the break room.

That's when it hit me: influence cuts both ways. One group pulled me toward cynicism. One person pulled me toward growth. Both had no official power over me—but both shaped me.

The best kind of influence, I realized, is the kind that leaves people stronger than it found them.

The Campfire Leader's Role in Creating Future Leaders

Your job isn't just to be a great leader. It's to create them.

Anyone can build a team of followers. A Campfire Leader builds a **bench of leaders**—people who think critically, lead confidently, and multiply impact.

Too often, traditional leadership looks like herding sheep. Safe. Controlled. Obedient. But sheep don't lead flocks.

A Campfire Leader nurtures lions.

I was once leading a small team on a project that was bigger than anything we'd handled before. Deadlines were tight, expectations were high, and the easy path would have been for me to keep a tight grip on every decision.

But I noticed one of my team members, James, had a sharp eye for strategy and a natural ability to earn people's trust. Instead of keeping him in the background, I asked him to lead a client meeting on his own. I told him, *"I'll be here if you need me, but this is your show."*

He was nervous, but he rose to the challenge. He didn't just deliver—he owned it. Over the next few months, I continued to give him opportunities, including leading calls, presenting updates, and coaching others. By the time the project wrapped, James wasn't just a solid contributor—he was a leader in his own right.

That experience changed me. I realized my job wasn't to be the hero of every story. My job was to create more heroes. A Campfire Leader doesn't just build a team of followers; they build a bench of future leaders, ready to carry the flame forward.

Lead With the Intent to Influence

Don't just lead because it's your role. Lead because it's your **responsibility** to influence others positively—whether they're watching or not.

Influence happens:

- When you show up consistently
- When you model calm under pressure
- When you admit a mistake
- When you help someone shine

Influence is often silent—but it's never small.

Years ago, I was managing a team during a particularly stressful quarter. Deadlines were piling up, a client was unhappy, and I felt the pressure more than I let on. One afternoon, I walked into the office to find my team looking frazzled and overwhelmed.

I took a deep breath, reminded myself that all eyes were on me, and said, *"We're going to get through this. Let's break it down into what we can control today."* We mapped out a plan, tackled the work piece by piece, and by the end of the week, we were back on track.

A few months later, one of my newer employees pulled me aside. She said, *"That day when everything felt like it was falling apart—you stayed calm. That's when I knew I could trust you."*

I hadn't even realized she was watching that closely. But that's the power of influence. It isn't always about grand speeches or big gestures. Sometimes it's in how you show up under pressure, how you admit mistakes, or how you help others shine. Influence is often quiet, but it leaves a lasting mark that outlasts authority.

Lead Ideas, Not Just People

People fade. Titles shift. But ideas? **Ideas live on.**

If you lead only for the moment, your leadership dies with the meeting. But when you lead through **vision**, your impact outlives your calendar.

Influence ensures your mission continues to march forward, even after you're gone.

Soon after starting Magnovo, my sales team was struggling with rejections, and morale was sinking fast. One morning, instead of another pep talk about closing deals, I wrote three words on the board that I had learned from one of my mentors: *"Relationships before revenue."*

I told the team, *"If we take care of people, the numbers will take care of themselves."* It wasn't a speech, just a simple reminder.

Years later, I ran into one of those former team members at a conference. He said, *"You know, I still use that phrase — 'relationships before revenue.' It's how I train new hires as a sales manager at my company.''*

That moment stopped me in my tracks. I had led my team through that difficult time, but I had also led an *idea* that continued to work long after I was gone.

That's the beauty of leading ideas, not just people. People fade. Titles shift. But the right idea? It keeps marching forward, carrying your influence with it.

How to Grow Your Influence

Let's get tactical. Here are the Campfire Leader tools for shaping future leaders:

1. Be Different (in the Best Way)

Don't try to fit in—stand out for the right reasons. Be the calm in chaos. The kind voice in a room full of critique. The reliable one when the storm hits.

People are influenced by those who live their values boldly.

My favorite show growing up was "Mr. Rogers' Neighborhood." In an era of loud, flashy television, Fred Rogers chose a different path. While children's programming was filled with slapstick humor and fast-paced entertainment, Rogers sat down, looked straight into the camera, and spoke slowly, gently, and sincerely to kids. He sang songs about feelings, put on cardigans, and taught lessons about kindness and empathy.

He didn't try to fit in—he stood out for the right reasons. In a noisy world, he was the calm in chaos. In an industry chasing ratings, he chose consistency, patience, and care. His influence came not from volume, but from values lived boldly.

Generations of children—and adults—were shaped by his quiet example. Rogers proved that you don't have to be the loudest voice in the room to be the one people remember. You just have to be different in the best way: the one who chooses kindness when it's easier to criticize, calm when it's easier to panic, and authenticity when it's easier to perform.

2. Build Trust Every Day

Trust is your most valuable leadership currency. Earn it through:

- Transparency
- Follow-through
- Integrity

"Say what you mean and mean what you say."
—Stephanie Lahart

Trust lets your words stick, even after you've left the room.

When Howard Schultz was leading Starbucks, he understood that coffee wasn't the company's only product—*trust* was. From the beginning, he emphasized transparency with employees and follow-through with customers.

During the 2008 financial crisis, Starbucks struggled. Stores were closing, profits were down, and morale was shaken. Instead of hiding behind corporate spin, Schultz stood in front of employees and shareholders and acknowledged the challenges openly. He admitted mistakes, laid out a clear plan, and committed to specific actions—like retraining baristas to refocus on quality and temporarily shutting down stores to reset standards.

Those decisions weren't easy, but they built trust. Employees saw that he meant what he said, and customers noticed the renewed integrity in every cup. Starbucks not only recovered but became stronger, in large part because Schultz built trust one day at a time—through honesty, consistency, and integrity.

Trust, once earned, became the company's strongest currency. And even years later, Schultz's influence stuck because his words were backed by action.

I once worked under a manager named Paul. He wasn't the most charismatic leader, and he didn't give big speeches. But he had one quality that set him apart: if Paul said he was going to do something, you could count on it happening.

If he promised to review your proposal by Friday, it was in your inbox by Thursday afternoon. If he told a client he'd call at 3:00, the phone rang at 2:59. And if he admitted a mistake—which he did openly—he was the first to own it and fix it.

What I didn't realize at the time was how much trust that built in our team. We didn't second-guess him. We didn't hedge our words. We trusted his consistency, which gave us the confidence to move faster and make decisions without hesitation.

Paul showed me that trust isn't earned in grand gestures—it's built brick by brick, day after day, through transparency, follow-through, and integrity. He lived out the saying: *"Say what you mean and mean what you say."*

3. Empower Others

Empowerment is influence in action. Tell people what they do well. Give them ownership. Let them make mistakes and recover stronger.

When you empower someone, you don't just impact their work—you rewrite their story.

Phil Jackson, the legendary NBA coach of the Chicago Bulls and Los Angeles Lakers, is often remembered for winning 11 championships. But his real genius wasn't just strategy—it was empowerment.

Jackson believed that great teams weren't built by centering one superstar, but by elevating the whole roster. With the Bulls, he empowered role players like Steve Kerr and Toni Kukoč to take big shots when the spotlight usually belonged to Michael Jordan. With the Lakers, he trusted Derek Fisher to lead huddles and encouraged younger players to speak up, even when Kobe Bryant and Shaquille O'Neal were on the floor.

By giving his players ownership, he did more than win games—he helped them grow into leaders themselves. Kerr later became a championship-winning coach, Fisher became a respected team leader, and countless others carried Jackson's lessons into their own careers.

Phil Jackson proved that empowerment is influence in action. By trusting his players to make decisions, learn from mistakes, and step into responsibility, he didn't just impact their performance—he rewrote their stories as leaders on and off the court.

4. Elevate the Room

Let your presence raise the standard. Elevate the tone, the expectations, the energy. Be the one who makes everyone better just by being around.

Influence is measured by what others do after you leave.

Several years ago, I hired a summer intern named Sarah. On paper, she was just a college student getting some experience. No title. No authority. But the moment she joined our meetings, something shifted.

She always came prepared—notes in hand, questions ready, and ideas thought through. She showed genuine curiosity, listened intently, and treated everyone with respect, no matter their role. Within weeks, I noticed the rest of the team stepping up. If Sarah was coming in that prepared, how could the rest of us show up halfway?

She didn't lecture anyone or demand higher standards. She simply modeled them. And when her internship ended, the habits she sparked—better preparation, sharper conversations, more respect in the room—stuck with us.

That's the true test of influence: what people do after you're gone. Sarah didn't just add value while she was in the office. She left a ripple effect that elevated our team long after she left.

5. Never Lead in Ignorance

Listen. Learn. Adapt. Nothing ruins influence like arrogance wrapped in a title. Leaders who ignore feedback or stay in an echo chamber lose the hearts of their people.

A Campfire Leader stays close enough to feel the heat—but far enough to let others grow.

At a company I worked with, we had a product manager named Lisa who was in charge of rolling out a new service line. The team tried to warn her that the timeline was too tight, the features weren't ready, and the customer research was incomplete. But Lisa wasn't interested in feedback—she had her plan, and she was determined to stick to it.

She pushed the launch forward anyway. On release day, customers immediately spotted glitches. Support lines lit up with complaints. Sales numbers lagged far behind projections. Instead of pausing to adapt, Lisa doubled down, insisting the team "just needed to sell harder."

The fallout was rough. The service had to be pulled back, the company's reputation took a hit, and team morale sank. The saddest part? The problems could have been avoided if Lisa had simply listened and adjusted.

Her title gave her authority, but her ignorance cost her influence. A Campfire Leader stays close enough to hear the truth, even when it's uncomfortable. Lisa chose not to—and lost the trust of her people in the process.

6. Motivate Without Manipulating

Motivation says: *"I believe in you."*
Manipulation says: *"I need you to believe in me."*

Keep your motives clear. Lead from hope, not fear. Uplift people, don't guilt them.

Tony Dungy, former NFL coach of the Indianapolis Colts, is a clear example of motivating without manipulating. Known for his calm, steady demeanor, Dungy never resorted to fear, yelling, or guilt to get his players to perform. Instead, he built trust through encouragement, consistency, and belief in his team.

Dungy's philosophy was simple: focus on character, preparation, and resilience. He reminded his players that their worth wasn't defined by a single game, but by how they carried themselves every day. When the Colts finally won the Super Bowl in 2007, many players credited Dungy's influence—not just his playbook. He motivated them by saying, in effect, *"I believe in you,"* and his team responded by believing in themselves.

Dungy proved that leaders don't need to manipulate to get results. By leading from hope instead of fear, he built a culture of respect and resilience that outlasted his own coaching career.

7. Combine Leadership + Influence

You don't have to choose between being a strong leader and an effective influencer. You need both.

Influence without leadership can lack direction. Leadership without influence lacks loyalty.

When combined, they build teams that are:

- Loyal but not dependent
- Brave but not reckless
- Growing but still grounded

A few years ago, I consulted with a large regional healthcare company. On paper, they had plenty of leaders—directors, managers, supervisors—all with clear authority. But when I asked employees what leadership felt like, I kept hearing the same words: *"strict," "structured," "top-down."*

People followed directions, but they weren't inspired. They clocked in, did their work, and clocked out. Leadership was there, but influence was missing.

During our workshops, we focused on helping their managers move beyond just managing tasks. I encouraged them to ask more questions, to listen for what their teams weren't saying, and to celebrate small wins out loud. At the same time, I worked with them to set clearer expectations, communicate priorities, and hold people accountable.

The shift was striking. Within months, staff started describing their leaders differently. Instead of *"They tell us what to do,"* I heard *"They believe in us."* Instead of hesitation, I saw initiative. One department even reported its best quarter in years, not because the process had changed, but because the people felt empowered to take ownership of it.

That's the sweet spot. Authority gave the leaders direction. Influence gave them loyalty. Together, they built teams that were loyal yet not dependent, brave yet not reckless, growing yet still grounded.

That company didn't just learn to lead people—they learned to lead with influence. And that made all the difference.

Create Leaders, Not Just Results

Anyone can hit a number or complete a project. That's management.

But creating someone who's **stronger, wiser, more confident** because of your leadership? That's legacy.

You're not just here to lead today. You're here to **light someone else's torch for tomorrow.**

Quick Check: Are You Influencing or Controlling?

Ask yourself:

- Do people feel braver or smaller after talking to me?
- Do I create space for input—or only space for agreement?
- Do I teach people how to think or tell them what to do?
- Do I correct in private and celebrate in public?

Your answers say more about your influence than any performance review.

The Final Test of Influence

Here's the true measure of your leadership:

If your team had to operate without you for a week, would they survive—or would they soar?

Campfire Leaders don't create dependence. They build independence. They create ecosystems that thrive without their constant control.

Because influence, not control, is the true art of leadership.

In the next (and final) chapter, we'll tie it all together. We'll talk about the type of leadership that doesn't just manage or direct—but **lasts**.

Chapter 10 – Conclusion

"Leadership is communicating others' worth and potential so clearly that they are inspired to see it in themselves."
—Stephen Covey

There's a fine line between being a leader... and becoming a dictator.

And it's thinner than most people think.

Once you're in a position of authority, it becomes dangerously easy to slide from guiding people to controlling them. From lighting the way to blinding the path.

But let's get one thing clear: Campfire Leaders don't control. They inspire.

Dictators Burn Bridges. Campfire Leaders Build Them.

As we have shown in this book, history has no shortage of individuals who misused power and led entire teams, nations, or organizations into ruin. Why? Because they led with fear. They crushed creativity. They took up space instead of making room.

A dictator issues commands.
A Campfire Leader offers clarity.

A dictator blames others.
A Campfire Leader takes responsibility.

A dictator demands loyalty.
A Campfire Leader earns trust.

If someone bosses people around, micromanages everything, and never takes responsibility for their mistakes, you're not looking at a leader. You're staring into the flames of a leadership burnout.

Pride vs. Arrogance

Pride can be a healthy thing. It says, *"I'm doing something worthwhile."*
Arrogance whispers, *"I'm better than everyone here."*

The difference is humility.

A Campfire Leader stands tall—but never stands above. They walk alongside their people, not in front of them. They inspire others to rise, not bow down.

Leadership Is a Verb, Not a Title

Leadership isn't a label you wear. It's a legacy you live.

Too many people think a title means they've arrived. Their job is to instruct, correct, and protect.

But real leadership? It serves, grows, and ignites.

It's rolling up your sleeves, listening first, and leaving every person better than you found them.

Campfire Leaders Are Motivators, Not Managers

They don't just say, "Here's the task." They ask, "Here's the goal—how do you want to help us get there?"

They don't manage output. They motivate ownership.

Because when people feel seen, heard, and valued, they go from checking boxes to chasing excellence.

Fear Is a Terrible Fuel

Sure, you can lead with fear. You might even get results.

But you'll lose:

- Creativity
- Loyalty
- Well-being
- Respect

Fear disconnects the brain from purpose. It stirs anxiety, not ambition.

A Campfire Leader doesn't burn people out—they light people up.

Create More Leaders, Not More Dependents

Some leaders secretly love when their teams rely on them for everything. It strokes the ego. It feels powerful.

But a Campfire Leader knows that real success is when the team can operate—and even thrive—without them.

Trust your people enough to lead.
Let them try. Let them fail. Let them grow.

The Trust Loop: It Goes Both Ways

We talk a lot about employees needing to trust leaders. But here's the truth:

Leaders must trust their teams too.

- Trust them to make smart decisions.
- Trust them to admit mistakes.
- Trust them to take initiative.

Micromanagement crushes growth. Empowerment expands it.

Flexibility Isn't Weakness—It's Wisdom

You don't lead robots. You lead humans.

People have strengths, limits, and different ways of reaching the same goal. A Campfire Leader adapts. They know when to challenge someone and when to offer grace.

When you meet people where they are, you help them rise to where they need to be.

Shift from "My Decision" to "Our Decision"

Dictators isolate decision-making. Campfire Leaders **collaborate**.

They ask:

- "What do you think?"
- "What might we try differently?"
- "What would make this better?"

Shared decisions lead to shared ownership—and better outcomes.

Culture Is Contagious

If your office feels heavy, tense, or cold, it didn't happen by accident.

Culture follows the leader.

A Campfire Leader brings warmth. They create a space where people are free to think, speak, and contribute. They know that positivity isn't fluff—it's fuel.

If your team environment feels toxic, check the thermostat: it starts with you.

Friendliness Has Boundaries. Professionalism Has Standards.

Being liked is nice. Being respected is better.

You can be approachable without being everyone's best friend. You can joke without losing your edge. **The trick is clarity: people need to know where the line is.**

A Campfire Leader is warm, but grounded. Friendly, but firm. Professional, without being pretentious.

Appreciation: The Most Underused Superpower

A "thank you" can shift a week.
Recognition can reignite a burned-out teammate.
A small reward can lead to a big breakthrough.

People don't just want money. They want meaning.

You don't need a budget to make someone feel valued. Just say it. And mean it.

You Don't Have to Be Perfect—Just Present

Some leaders crumble under pressure. They think they must have all the answers.

But guess what?

People don't follow perfection.
They follow presence.
They follow steadiness.
They follow humility.

It's okay not to know everything. Just be honest, be calm, and keep showing up.

Ditch the Blame Game. Build the Team Game.

When something goes wrong, bad leaders look for a scapegoat.

Campfire Leaders look for a solution—and start with themselves.

Accountability should never be a weapon. It's a tool for **growth**, not **guilt**.

The Three R's of Campfire Leadership: Respect, Recognition, Reward

These are your anchors. Every team needs them.

- **Respect**: Treat everyone like they matter—because they do.
- **Recognition**: Let people know you see their efforts, not just their outcomes.
- **Reward**: Celebrate progress, not just perfection.

You'll be amazed at how fast your team grows when they feel like they belong.

The Final Flame

I'm finishing the book back where it started…Alaska. Every couple of years, I join one of my closest friends of almost 50 years in the world and his wife at their cabin in Seldovia, Alaska. Lance and Brooke have been coming here for over 30 years. It's a sleepy little town that only has 300 residents.

It's not easy to get to. You first fly to Anchorage. Then you either drive 5 hours or fly a prop plane to Homer, Alaska. Finally, you either take a ferry or a smaller prop plane over the bay to Seldovia. It is a fantastic place to visit.

Here I'm able to get away from the busyness of the world and recharge. I take time to reflect on the decisions of my life and career. I can't emphasize to you how important it is to get away and reconnect with nature. The few weeks I stay here give me the time I need to focus on what is important to me and plan my next steps in my life and career. I find that I can't be the Campfire Leader that I should be unless I have taken time to relax and focus. That's what trips back to Alaska do for me. I get to relax, hike, and especially fish.

I've already caught my share of salmon this trip, just like my father, siblings, and I did over 50 years ago. I get to fish on the streams, lakes, and rivers that I fished when I was a kid. On a very personal note, "I miss you, Dad., I wish you were here with me."

Let's bring it full circle.

Campfire Leadership isn't just a philosophy. It's a **practice.**
A choice you make every day.

It's about being:

- Warm, not wishy-washy
- Strong, but not stiff
- Bright, without burning out

It's about lighting the way so others can walk boldly into theirs.

You don't need to be the loudest in the room. Just be the one who listens.
You don't need to have all the answers. Just ask better questions.

You don't need to carry the whole fire. Just spark it, and let it spread.

Be the leader you once needed.
Be the leader you wish you had.
Be the Campfire Leader who makes others believe they can lead, too.

Now go and light the way.

The Campfire Leadership Workbook & Journal

This isn't just a workbook.

It's a spark. A mirror. A guide for the kind of leader you're becoming—not just at work, but in life.

You're not here by accident.
Something in you wants to lead with more clarity, connection, and purpose.

And that's exactly what this journey is about.

As you turn these pages, you'll uncover your strengths, challenge your habits, and light the path for others. Don't worry about perfect answers, just show up honestly. The campfire grows with every insight, every story, every moment of reflection.

If you'd like to explore this further, discuss it with your team, or simply share your experience, I'd love to connect.

Visit **magnovo.com or campfireleadership.com**
 Or email me directly at **rob.jackson@magnovo.com**

Now—take a deep breath, pick up your pen, and let's build a fire worth gathering around.

Welcome to the Workbook

Welcome to the Campfire Leadership Workbook & Journal!

This companion guide is your personal space to grow, reflect, and ignite the leader within you. Inspired by the Campfire Leadership philosophy, this workbook will help you uncover your leadership style, identify your strengths, and develop new strategies to become a well-rounded, trusted leader.

You'll explore the four leadership styles—Torch, Spotlight, Disco Light, and Lighthouse—through quizzes, prompts, activities, and challenges designed to stretch and support you. Whether you're guiding a team, starting your journey, or lighting the path for others, this workbook will fuel your fire and focus your influence.

Leadership isn't about having all the answers, it's about building a fire others want to gather around. Let this be your space to tend that fire.

And as you go, don't just reflect—track your progress. Below, you'll find a Leadership Challenge Tracker to help you document what you're learning, when you started each challenge, and what insights you gained along the way.

Section 1: Find Your Flame – Leadership Style Quiz

Instructions: For each question, choose the answer that best describes how you most often lead. Select only one answer per question.

1. When leading a team project, I prefer to:

- A. Be steady and reliable.
- B. Make quick, confident decisions.
- C. Inspire the group with energy.
- D. Organize the details and build a plan.

2. When conflict arises, I tend to:

- A. Keep the peace and support others emotionally.
- B. Address it head-on.
- C. Try to lighten the mood and redirect the energy.
- D. Analyze the root cause before reacting.

3. In meetings, I usually:

- A. Listen carefully and offer support.
- B. Drive the agenda forward quickly.
- C. Engage with humor and enthusiasm.
- D. Ask thoughtful, clarifying questions.

4. My team sees me as:

- A. Reliable and caring.
- B. Bold and results-oriented.
- C. Charismatic and fun.
- D. Smart and precise.

5. When making decisions, I:

- A. Consult with others to maintain harmony.
- B. Decide quickly and move forward.
- C. Seek input in a lively group conversation.
- D. Research and analyze before acting.

6. Under pressure, I tend to:

- A. Stay calm and help others stay grounded.
- B. Take charge and lead with urgency.
- C. Use positivity to motivate others.
- D. Focus on facts and processes.

7. My favorite part of leadership is:

- A. Building strong relationships.
- B. Driving toward big goals.
- C. Energizing and connecting people.
- D. Solving complex problems.

8. Others might criticize me for:

- A. Avoiding conflict.
- B. Being too direct or intense.
- C. Being too scattered or unrealistic.
- D. Overthinking or being inflexible.

9. I feel most energized when:

- A. People feel safe and supported.
- B. We meet a tough challenge.
- C. Everyone is engaged and having fun.
- D. Things are organized and under control.

10. When I give feedback, I try to:

- A. Be kind and encouraging.
- B. Be direct and focused.
- C. Uplift and energize the person.
- D. Be specific and factual.

11. I prefer to work:

- A. On steady, collaborative teams.
- B. On fast-moving, high-achieving teams.
- C. On creative, dynamic teams.
- D. On well-structured, detail-oriented teams.

12. My communication style is:

- A. Calm and supportive.
- B. Clear and assertive.
- C. Enthusiastic and expressive.
- D. Thoughtful and measured.

13. In uncertain times, I:

- A. Help others feel reassured.
- B. Take charge and act quickly.
- C. Stay optimistic and energize the team.
- D. Plan for multiple scenarios.

14. When I delegate, I:

- A. Offer guidance and check in regularly.
- B. Set expectations and expect results.
- C. Empower with excitement and praise.
- D. Provide detailed instructions.

15. My biggest strength is:

- A. Loyalty and dependability.
- B. Courage and decisiveness.
- C. Passion and inspiration.
- D. Discipline and intelligence.

16. My biggest leadership fear is:

- A. Letting people down.
- B. Being seen as weak.
- C. Being ignored or misunderstood.
- D. Making a mistake or losing control.

17. I prefer praise that:

- A. Acknowledges my support.
- B. Recognizes my leadership.
- C. Celebrates my energy.
- D. Highlights my accuracy.

18. I would rather lead by:

- A. Example and quiet strength.
- B. Direction and determination.
- C. Connection and excitement.
- D. Systems and expertise.

19. People trust me because I:

- A. Am consistent and loyal.
- B. Get results.
- C. Make them feel good.
- D. Am prepared and logical.

20. My ideal leadership legacy is:

- A. "They always had my back."
- B. "They moved mountains."
- C. "They made me believe in myself."
- D. "They helped us build something that lasts."

How to Score Your Results

Count how many times you chose each letter:

- **A** = Torch Leader (DISC: Steady – S)
- **B** = Spotlight Leader (DISC: Dominant – D)
- **C** = Disco Light Leader (DISC: Influence – I)
- **D** = Lighthouse Leader (DISC: Conscientious – C)

Tally Your Answers:

Letter	Style	Tally
A	Torch Leader	_____
B	Spotlight Leader	_____
C	Disco Light Leader	_____
D	Lighthouse Leader	_____

Score Range Guide:

- 13–20 = Strongly aligned
- 9–12 = Moderately aligned
- 5–8 = Occasionally shows up
- Even spread? You may be a *Campfire Leader*—flexible and situationally aware.

Use the following to interpret your result:

Torch Leader (Mostly A's)

You lead with loyalty, calm, and consistency. Your quiet strength makes others feel safe and supported.

Spotlight Leader (Mostly B's)

You lead with boldness, direction, and drive. People follow your energy and decisive momentum.

Disco Light Leader (Mostly C's)

You lead with enthusiasm, charisma, and optimism. You lift others up and bring contagious energy.

Lighthouse Leader (Mostly D's)

You lead with preparation, wisdom, and structure. Your steady guidance helps others navigate complexity.

Balanced Result

If you have an even distribution across styles, you may be a Campfire Leader—someone who adapts to multiple styles depending on the situation.

Let this quiz guide your journaling, challenges, and reflection as you develop your leadership fire.

Section 2: Fuel the Fire – Guided Journal Prompts

Weekly Reflection Prompts (Repeat Weekly)

Reflect on these each week. Leave space to write your responses.

1. What leadership moment stood out to you this week?

2. When did you act out of alignment with your leadership values?

_____

_____

_____

_____

_____

_____

_____

_____

3. What feedback did you receive? How did you respond?

_____

_____

_____

_____

_____

_____

_____

_____

_____

_____

4. Who did you influence this week—and how?

_____

_____

_____

_____

_____

Style-Specific Reflection Prompts

Use the section that matches your primary leadership style, or explore all four to grow your versatility.

Torch Leader Prompts *(Steady – S style)*

1. Where did you show quiet strength this week?

_____

_____

2. What tension or conflict did you avoid that might need revisiting?

_____

_____

3. How did you support someone without needing recognition?

_____

_____

4. What boundaries did you set (or fail to set), and what did you learn?

_____

_____

Spotlight Leader Prompts *(Dominant – D style)*

1. Did your drive overshadow a teammate's voice?

2. What bold move did you make—and what did you learn?

3. How did you handle disagreements or pushback this week?

4. Did your urgency help or hurt team morale?

Disco Light Leader Prompts *(Influence – I style)*

1. How did your energy influence your team's morale?

_____

_____

2. Did you overcommit? If so, how can you refocus?

_____

_____

3. What conversation did you steer with positivity that needed more depth?

_____

_____

4. Who did you make feel seen or celebrated this week?

_____

_____

Lighthouse Leader Prompts *(Conscientious – C style)*

1. Where did your preparation pay off?

_____

_____

2. Did your pursuit of perfection prevent progress?

_____

_____

3. What decision took too long—and how could you streamline next time?

_____

_____

4. How did you use your expertise to empower someone else?

_____

_____

Section 3: Building the Campfire – Leadership Tools

Leadership Style Integration Map

Use this quick-reference guide to help flex into other leadership modes:

From → To	When to Flex
Torch → Spotlight	When a firm, fast decision is needed.
Spotlight → Lighthouse	When details, accuracy, or long-term thinking is crucial.
Disco Light → Torch	When your team needs calm more than charisma.
Lighthouse → Disco	When human connection matters more than perfect execution.

Campfire Leadership Weekly Tracker

Use this weekly checklist to stay intentional with your leadership presence:

- I listened more than I spoke.
- I invited feedback.
- I recognized someone else's effort.
- I delegated something I usually control.
- I showed up aligned with my core values.
- I took a moment to pause and reflect before reacting.

Use the table on the following page to track your mental health and resilience over several weeks.

Rate your energy, focus, and stress levels, and note any contributing factors.

Legend:

- **Energy**: Are you charged or drained?
- **Focus**: Are you dialed in or scattered?
- **Stress**: Are you managing, tolerating, or drowning?
- **Notes**: What factors are fueling or draining your fire?

Mental Wellbeing Monitor (Weekly Table)

Week #	Energy	Focus	Stress	What's Helping or Hurting?
	Full/Half/Empty		Calm/Mid/Overwhelmed	
1				
2				
3				
4				
5				
6				

Section 4: Leadership Challenge Series (6 Months)

Each month, take on one leadership challenge. These are designed to help you grow, lean into your strengths, and lead more intentionally. Reflect in writing after each challenge using the space provided.

Month 1: Lead From Your Strength

Theme: Amplify your natural leadership style

This month is all about recognizing what you do best—and then doing more of it on purpose. Whether you're a Torch, Spotlight, Disco Light, or Lighthouse leader, your strength can become someone else's breakthrough. Each week builds on the last.

Week 1 – Recognize & Reflect

Identify your **dominant leadership style** and commit to leading from it intentionally this week. Don't apologize for it—amplify it.

What is your dominant style?

☐ Torch   ☐ Spotlight   ☐ Disco Light   ☐ Lighthouse

Journal Prompt:
How did leading from your strength elevate the people around you?

_____

_____

Week 2 – Adjust & Align

Reflect on what went well and what didn't. Now make minor adjustments. Did you overuse your strength? Did it spark new opportunities? Did you get feedback?

Journal Prompt:
What do I need to adjust or refine in how I use my strength?

_____

_____

Week 3 – Share & Stretch

Find a moment to **intentionally use your strength to serve someone else's leadership journey**—mentor, support, coach, or simply encourage.

Journal Prompt:
Who did I help grow by leveraging my strengths?

_____

_____

Week 4 – Reflect & Reinforce

Zoom out. Reflect on the whole month. How are you different? How did others respond? What about this style do you now understand or appreciate better?

Journal Prompt:
 What has this month taught me about myself—and what will I carry forward?

_____

_____

Month 2: Tend the Quiet Flame

Theme: Uplift someone else's leadership potential

This month is about using your leadership presence to **shine a light on someone else**. Many people go unnoticed not because they lack value, but because they lack visibility. Campfire Leaders don't just lead loudly, they lead intentionally.

Week 1 – Identify the Quiet Flame

Observe your team or network. Who contributes behind the scenes? Who shows up consistently but quietly? Choose one person to focus on this month.

Journal Prompt:
Who have I overlooked—or seen others overlook—and why might they need support right now?

Week 2 – Speak Life Into Their Contribution

This week, give intentional encouragement. Privately or publicly, **recognize the person's work, ideas, or character**. Be sincere and specific.

Journal Prompt:
What words did I share—and how were they received?

Week 3 – Create a Spotlight Opportunity

Invite this person into a space where they can be seen—whether that's asking for their input in a meeting, delegating a meaningful task, or offering them a platform to lead.

Journal Prompt:
What opportunity did I create, and what happened?

Week 4 – Reflect on Growth (Theirs and Yours)

Reflect on the impact of your intentional attention. How did they grow? What did you learn about quiet leadership? How will you maintain this habit?

Journal Prompt:
What impact did I make by lifting up someone else's voice—and how did it grow *me*, too?

Month 3: Light the Next Torch

Theme: Mentor and multiply leadership

Leadership isn't just about being followed, it's about creating more leaders. This month, intentionally choose someone to invest in. Whether they're new to leadership or just need a nudge of belief, *your fire can light theirs*.

Week 1 – Choose & Commit to a Future Leader

Consider someone who shows potential but may require encouragement, guidance, or space to develop. Reach out, let them know you see something in them, and offer to walk alongside them.

Journal Prompt:
Who did I choose to mentor, and why?

Week 2 – Listen, Encourage, Empower

This week, focus less on giving advice and more on listening. Ask good questions. Share encouragement. Help them clarify their goals and build confidence.

Journal Prompt:
What conversations opened up—and what did I learn about their potential?

Week 3 – Create a Real Opportunity to Lead

Give them a real chance to step forward. Assign a task, invite them to present, let them lead part of a project, or ask them to mentor someone else.

Journal Prompt:
What opportunity did I create—and how did they show up?

Week 4 – Reflect on the Ripple

Leadership is contagious. This week, reflect on how your mentorship affected them, and what it sparked in you.

Journal Prompt:

What did I learn by sharing my leadership fire with someone else?

_____

_____

_____

_____

_____

_____

_____

_____

Month 4: Shine Brighter in Your Strength

Theme: Elevate your leadership where it hasn't been seen before

You've identified your dominant leadership style. This month, it's time to **amplify it in a new context**. Whether that's with a different team, on a new project, or in your personal life—take what you're great at and shine it into unfamiliar territory.

Week 1 – Define a New Space to Show Up In

Where have you been holding back your natural leadership style? Choose a new environment—outside your comfort zone—where your strength could make a real impact.

Journal Prompt:
Where am I needed—but not yet fully showing up?

Week 2 – Step Forward, Boldly and Intentionally

This week, take action. Speak up in that meeting. Volunteer for that stretch assignment. Initiate that conversation. Let your strength be seen and felt.

Journal Prompt:
 What action did I take to expand my presence—and how did others respond?

_____

_____

_____

Week 3 – Invite Feedback or Partnership

Reach out to someone in that new space. Ask for feedback, collaboration, or support. Use your strength *with* others, not just around them.

Journal Prompt:
 How did collaboration or feedback refine my strength?

_____

_____

_____

Week 4 – Reflect on What You've Grown Into

You've stretched. You've shown up. Now reflect on what's changed—not just around you, but *within you*.

Journal Prompt:
What new possibilities emerged when I elevated my best self?

_____

_____

_____

_____

_____

_____

Month 5: Build a Feedback Loop

Theme: Listen to grow

Leadership without feedback is like trying to lead in the dark. This month is about **inviting reflection, not correction**—and using the insights from others to become a more trusted, aware, and adaptable leader.

Week 1 – Identify & Invite Honest Voices

Choose at least three people: one peer, one direct report, and one mentor/supervisor (if applicable). Let them know you're asking for **authentic, constructive feedback**—not flattery.

Journal Prompt:
Who did I ask for feedback, and why did I choose them?

_____

_____

Week 2 – Ask the Right Questions

Use open-ended prompts like:

- "What's one thing I do well that I should do more of?"
- "What's one behavior I could change to be a better leader for you?"
  Document their responses **without defensiveness**.

Journal Prompt:
 What did I hear—and what surprised me?

_____

_____

Week 3 – Analyze the Patterns

Look across all feedback for recurring themes. Are there blind
spots? Strengths I've underused? Gaps between how I see myself
and how others experience me?

Journal Prompt:
 What patterns did I notice—and what truth do they reveal?

_____

_____

_____

_____

_____

Week 4 – Act on What Matters Most

Choose one insight to implement this week. Keep it simple and
visible. Then let the people who gave you feedback know how
you're acting on it.

Journal Prompt:

What did I do differently—and how did it feel?

_____

_____

_____

_____

_____

_____

Month 6: Create a Personal Leadership Guide

Theme: Define your leadership philosophy

This month is about reflection, clarity, and ownership. You've spent months growing, mentoring, adjusting, and showing up with intention. Now it's time to **capture your leadership voice** in a way that can guide you—and inspire others.

Week 1 – Reflect on Your Journey

Look back at the last 5 months. What's changed in how you lead? What insights or "aha moments" stuck with you the most?

Journal Prompt:
What have I learned about myself as a leader through this process?

_____

_____

_____

Week 2 – Identify Your Core Beliefs

Write down 3–5 core leadership beliefs. These should reflect *how* you want to lead, not just what you want to accomplish.

Examples:

- "I believe leadership is earned through trust, not titles."
- "I believe in progress over perfection."
- "I believe in leading with both strength and softness."

Journal Prompt:
What do I believe about leadership—and why?

_____

_____

_____

Week 3 – Draft Your Leadership Manifesto

Using your beliefs, values, and experiences, write a short (1-page or less) **Leadership Manifesto**. This is your "North Star"—something you can revisit, share, or even post in your office.

Journal Prompt:
What words, phrases, or ideas must be part of my manifesto?

_____

_____

_____

Week 4 – Share It. Live It. Evolve It.

Share your manifesto with someone you trust—a team member, mentor, or coach. Ask them: *"Does this sound like me?"* Commit to reviewing and revising it every 6–12 months as you grow.

Journal Prompt:
What feedback did I receive—and how will I keep this manifesto alive?

_____

_____

_____

Section 5: Reflection and Legacy Pages

Take your time with these. They're meant to be reflective, personal, and deeply meaningful. Come back to them as you grow.

My Leadership Mission Statement

What do you stand for as a leader? What do you want people to experience when they work with you?

_____

_____

_____

_____

_____

_____

_____

_____

My Top 3 Campfire Values

What values fuel your fire and guide your leadership?

1. _____

_____

2. _____

_____

3. _____

_____

Why do these matter to you?

_____

_____

_____

_____

_____

_____

_____

_____

How I Want to Be Remembered as a Leader

What do you hope others say about you when you're not in the room—or long after you've left the team?

Top 10 Leadership Moments of the Year

Think of wins, growth, breakthroughs, or challenges you overcame.

1. _____

_____

2. _____

_____

3. _____

_____

4. _____

_____

5. _____

_____

6. _____

_____

7. _____

_____

8. _____

_____

9. _____

_____

10. _____

_____

The Leader I Once Needed... and Now Strive to Be

Think of a moment when you felt unseen, unsupported, or misunderstood. Who did you need then? Now describe how you're becoming that person for others.

_____

_____

_____

_____

_____

_____

_____

_____

_____

Bonus Section: Campfire Circles - Group

Discussion Prompts

- Which style is most misunderstood—and why?
- When has someone's warmth made you feel safe to grow?
- What does healthy conflict look like in our workplace?
- How do we build trust when things go wrong?

Leadership Challenge Tracker

Month	Challenge Focus	Date Started	Date Completed	Key Insights / Takeaways
Month 1	Lead From Your Strength			
Month 2	Tend the Quiet Flame			
Month 3	Light the Next Torch			
Month 4	Shine Brighter in Your Strength			

Leadership Challenge Tracker

Month	Challenge Focus	Date Started	Date Completed	Key Insights / Takeaways
Month 5	Build a Feedback Loop			
Month 6	Create a Personal Leadership Guide			

Conclusion: The Fire Doesn't Go Out Here

You've done more than complete a workbook; you've tended a fire.

Over the past weeks and months, you've reflected, stretched, led with purpose, and discovered what kind of leader the world truly needs. You've amplified your strengths, lifted others up, and lit the path forward—not just for yourself, but for those around you.

But Campfire Leadership doesn't end here.

Leadership is never a checklist; it's a calling. It lives in the daily moments: the pause before you speak, the courage to coach, the decision to trust, the choice to grow. The fire you've built needs tending. It needs purpose. And it needs people.

So, keep tending the flame. Keep listening. Keep learning. And most of all—keep showing up with warmth, courage, and integrity.

Because the best leaders don't just burn bright.

They make it safe for others to shine as well.

About the Author

Rob Jackson has been the President of Magnovo Training Group for over 18 years, a company specializing in soft skills development training in leadership, presentation skills, team building, and communication. As an internationally requested keynote speaker and professional development trainer, he has traveled over a million miles around the globe training, but lives in Indianapolis, IN, with his wife of 38 years, and proudly hails from Salinas, CA.

Rob also enjoys traveling, fishing, scuba diving, and, most of all, making a difference in individuals' lives and careers by showing them what True Leadership looks like.

The *Campfire Leadership* workshop focuses on creating future leaders rather than merely followers. Rob has trained renowned individuals on how to lead as a Campfire Leader. After extensive research, he has concluded that leading as a Campfire leader is the most effective way to inspire others to walk beside you, rather than just following you.

If you are interested in learning more about the Campfire Leadership workshop, please visit **campfireleadership.com** and **magnovo.com**

Rob's first book *Campfire Leadership* is available on **amazon.com**

Additional Notes

Additional Notes

Additional Notes

Additional Notes

Additional Notes

Additional Notes

Additional Notes

www.ingramcontent.com/pod-product-compliance
Lightning Source LLC
Chambersburg PA
CBHW072144090426
42739CB00013B/3276